GRACE
ENTITLEMENTS
FROM
A LOVING FATHER

NORMAN WILSON

authorHOUSE®

AuthorHouse™
1663 Liberty Drive
Bloomington, IN 47403
www.authorhouse.com
Phone: 1 (800) 839-8640

Published by AuthorHouse   10/13/2015

ISBN: 978-1-5049-5614-7 (sc)
ISBN: 978-1-5049-5613-0 (e)

CONTENTS

ABOUT THE COVER

The Dance of Grace is not intended to be an illustration of a moment in the life of Jesus 2000 years ago, but rather a present depiction of the delight and celebration which He invites everyone to join in the present. I've chosen to portray Him dancing with children, for they come to him as they are, with no pretenses, with no performance or sense of duty. Looking in their eyes and knowing every decision they will ever make, whether good or bad, He laughs with delight because they are His. While onlookers watch, their hearts are stirred up to either desire to join the dance or to turn away, but the sheer joy and love that is seen captivates even the skeptic.

Too often we imagine we must "get ourselves in order" before we can experience his delight, but his call is simple: "Come to me and I will give . . ." Such is the meaning of Grace – when what we need is given freely. Not realizing our need keeps us from what Jesus said He came to do, "Bind up the broken hearted, proclaim freedom for the captives and to set the prisoners free." Do you recognize the chains? Do you feel the bondage from the lies? Do you want to be free? Let Him do as only He can—and join the celebration of His love and the Dance of Grace.

Mark Keathley – Artist

PREFACE

In our politically correct society the word "entitlement" has taken on a negative connotation because of its association with the so-called government entitlement programs. The dictionary lists as a definition for entitlement, "The condition of having a right to have, do, or get something." Another definition states, "The right to receive or do something." All who understand the marvelous grace of God realize that because of the unconditional love of God for us, He has provided through the finished work of His Son everything we need for life and godliness and declares they are ours as completely free entitlements.

CHAPTER ONE

Introduction

Every Christian has divine encounters with God. During my fifty-three years as a Christian I have been blessed my many divine encounters but two stand out as the most memorable. The first happened sometime during my thirtieth year. I don't recall the day or the month but remember the event very vividly. It came at a time in my life when I was struggling about whether I was a Christian or not. From the time I was fifteen I had assumed that I was a Christian because I had responded when an evangelist had said at the end of a service, "all who wish to go to heaven come up front." We were not church-goers so I had no previous knowledge of the Bible, heaven, or hell but assumed that heaven was better than hell. I watched as several of my classmates from school responded and so I went forward.

Those that met me must have thought that I knew for a person to go to heaven he must believe in Jesus as the Son of God. I say this because no one explained this to me; they just had me fill out a card and told me to come back on Sunday to be baptized. I was baptized (or rather dunked) the following Sunday, and went my way assuming I was a going to heaven. My relationship with the church soon after that experience basically ended until I was about twenty-eight. I became casually involved with the church for the next two years until I heard a minister say one Sunday that Jesus was a gentleman, that He would not save a person unless they wanted to be saved. I ran my experience with the church when I was fifteen through my mind; I could not recall ever saying that I believed in Jesus or acknowledged what He had done for me.

This became a nagging concern over the next several months. As I looked back over what had happened from when I was fifteen until I was thirty, it became obvious to me that God had been preparing me for my day of salvation. It was as if the Father said to the Holy Spirit on that night when I responded to the call, "See, he has indicated he wants to go to heaven, watch over him, and prepare him so that he will believe." That belief came by a divine encounter when the Holy Spirit made a house call, rousting me out of bed one evening with an urgency that I needed to acknowledge Jesus as my Savior. I responded to His invitation and my life has never been the same since.

The second memorable encounter came on August 7, 2010, when I was given a copy of Joseph Prince's book "Destined to Reign." Those that know Joseph Prince know that he is a radical preacher of the gospel of grace. I can truly say that I was captivated by the contents of that book. I approached Prince's book as I did other Christian books by validating his comments and Scripture interpretation by the Bible. The truths that began to emerge for me helped to clarify many applications of certain Scriptures. It soon became obvious to me that much of my misunderstanding of the Bible was because I was trying to live under both the Old and New Covenants. There had always been the questions about certain Old Testament Scriptures as to their application for the Christian. Through the study of this book and other Scriptures I became convinced that we as Gentiles were never under the Old Covenant; it was a covenant God made with Israel (Leviticus 26:46, Psalms 147:19-20, Romans 2:14-15).

The book also helped me understand the fact that no one after the time of Christ was under the Old Covenant because God had made it obsolete with the coming of the New Covenant (Hebrews 8:13).

This knowledge was a great breakthrough in interpreting and applying various Scriptures. The Holy Spirit used this book in two major ways, first, He took what Prince had written and used it as a catalyst to show me many other Scripture verses that explained the gospel of grace. The second thing that He did was to stir within me a quest to gain greater understanding about the wonderful grace of God. He led me to numerous grace preachers and writers that were instruments in teaching me more and more about grace. He ignited in me a desire to understand the scope of God's grace that continues to burn within me. The Scriptures have taken on new meanings as I examine them in the context of God's grace. I feel like I am currently at the kindergarten level in my knowledge and application of His grace.

The topic of grace is one of the simplest yet at the same time one of the most complex topics of the Scriptures. It is simple in its context regarding salvation, God has done it all and our response is to believe and receive it. Grace becomes very complex when we, as individuals, try to define it from our limited understanding and integrate it into our everyday activities, especially in the midst of a world system that endorses actions and attitudes devoid of grace.

Nearly every Christian regardless of his/her background will acknowledge their belief in the grace of God. Many, however, are unable to articulate beyond, "we are saved by grace," and "it is God's unmerited favor," a Biblical definition of grace. We can say that certainly both of these are true; it is not difficult to believe that God loves us and has by His grace forgiven us of all our sins. The difficulty emerges when we attempt to synchronize our limited understanding of grace with the various beliefs we have been taught regarding our association with God and sin. It becomes even more difficult when we try to manage our lives in a parameter of sin consciousness, sin awareness, and sin management taught by many religions, and often the church. Grace becomes relegated to a place of nebulous meaning, and is used carelessly in sermons and conversations.

The incorporation of grace into our daily activities and decisions is a lifelong learning process. It is a process of renewing our minds to the application of grace when confronted with life issues. It is easy to extend grace to others who are like us but it is a learning process to extend love and grace to those who are nothing like us, and those whose lifestyle embraces deviant activities. A Pharisaical interpretation and application of the Scriptures, which in most cases incorporates a mixture of the Old Covenant and the New Covenant, is a major cause of confusion in the understanding of true grace. We may enjoy a measure of the benefits of our relationship with Jesus without fully believing and applying those Scriptures that define who we truly are in Him, without experiencing the abundant life He has provided for us through His grace.

There is no lack in Jesus' desire to give mankind life and give it more abundantly. His generosity is expressed through His dealings with people as He modeled the Kingdom of God, and unveiled the heart of the Father toward mankind. His message of repentance was to encourage their transition from a lifestyle based upon performance to one of receiving what the Father had provided. His message to Israel to repent (change her thinking) in regards to her relationship and interaction with God is one that has resounded to all nations and people groups throughout every century. It especially addresses all religions of the world that have developed their own dogma and religious rituals of appeasing their version of a superior deity and attaining their version of paradise associated with Him.

Jesus' message of repentance was an invitation for Israel to abandon her dependency upon her own efforts and embrace the good news of His Kingdom where everything she needed would be provided for her. The message was, "It is not what you can do or must do for God, it is what God has already done for you and offers as a free gift that is received through belief in His Son." Jesus called it the gospel. It is a message of hope for a lost world.

The Christian is constantly being enticed away from the simplicity of the gospel of grace by the world, doctrines of other religions, and errors taught by the church. If a person lives within an atmosphere of unbiblical doctrinal beliefs long enough he may become acclimated to those beliefs and gradually compromise his own beliefs. In America all religions are tolerated and often given preference over Christianity in America's arena of political correctness.

This has created an environment where any religion, sect, cult, or the occult can find legitimacy and be given credence, causing confusion among unbelievers as to which is the right one to embrace for personal salvation and guidance in life matters. Our greatest safeguard against these erroneous beliefs and teachings is a Biblical understanding of the gospel of grace.

America is a melting pot of most of the religions of the world. The Western church as a rule has set guard against these damaging beliefs to keep them from infiltrating the church, but has often failed to grasp the great truths expressed in the gospel of grace that do not align with its own beliefs and practices.

Just a casual study of the many denominations, organizations, churches, sects, and religious groups that exist under the umbrella of "Christianity" will reveal that there is a broad spectrum of conflicting beliefs taught and followed. Many of these established doctrines have incorporated Old Covenant laws or a mixture of grace and law to be taught and practiced. This compromise of the true grace of God causes many to stumble and be in bondage to a performance mentality of Christianity rather than enjoying the freedoms grace brings.

This mixture of grace and Old Covenant law is deeply ingrained in the teachings and functions of much of the modern church. Very few evangelical Christians realize how deeply the law is embedded in their basic beliefs. Many teach that tongues and spiritual gifts are not a part of the New Testament Church while at the same time teaching that their members must keep the Ten Commandments, a part of an Old Covenant that the Bible declares to be obsolete.

Many evangelical churches teach that Jesus paid for all the sins of mankind when He died on the cross, but at the same time teach that if we don't forgive others that He will not forgive us. Both cannot be true. It seems to be double-mindedness to on the one hand teach that all our sins have been forgiven, and that we are the righteousness of God in Christ Jesus, while on the other hand teaching that we must confess our sins in order to be forgiven and cleansed of unrighteousness. Please do not think that I mean to devalue the act of forgiving others or the importance of acknowledging our wrongs to God. I just want to stress that God's forgiveness of our sins has nothing to do with our performance or whether we confess our sins or not. His forgiveness for sin is a once-for-all act of love for mankind. It's called the grace of God.

The mixture of the Old Covenant law and grace has its roots in the transition from the Old Covenant to the New Covenant and is embraced by many in the church due to a misunderstanding regarding the Christian's responsibility to the teachings of the Old Covenant. Paul's teachings focus on the attributes of the New Covenant and why the Old Covenant was no longer valid. He stressed the harms associated with mixing the two covenants. Yet, many in Paul's day succumbed to the pressures of law performance. Today, as clear as Paul's messages are in Romans and Galatians, many modern churches still mix the two, in some cases teaching that their members must outright follow the Old Covenant law. Tithing is just one example.

Most of the early revivalists and founding fathers of the Christian movement in America in their efforts to get men saved, and to instruct them in how to live righteous lives, mixed the two covenants in both their preaching and teaching. Out of these early movements denominations were formed that incorporated these beliefs into their doctrinal statements. Seminaries were founded to teach these tenets to those going into full-time Christian ministries.

Some of these seminaries and the denominations they represented would excommunicate a person for speaking in tongues while at the same time teaching that we are responsible to keep the tenets of the Law under the Old Covenant. Therefore, much of the Western church became, and is still, the cloning agent for developing Christians who hold fast to a mixture of Old and New Covenant beliefs.

This mixture robs Christians of their freedom provided through the finished work of Jesus Christ and places them in bondage to rules and regulations that Jesus died to free them from. Even those of us who believe in true Biblical grace are tempted to default back to the law or a mixture when confronted with difficult choices and issues because of what we were previously taught.

It should be evident that this mixture has left much of the modern church void of the power promised in the gospel, and has infiltrated the belief systems of most Christians. What is the solution? In the book of Revelation John wrote, "He that has an ear, let him hear what the Spirit says to the church." This is still valid advice for the modern church. It implies two things, that to hear the Spirit we must first have a relationship whereby we are listening to Him. Secondly, we must respond to what He is saying.

What is the Spirit saying to the Church? His message is the same as Jesus preached, "Repent for the Kingdom of God is at hand." Although the Kingdom was established with the coming of Jesus, the message of repentance remains valid. We are to change our minds regarding the gospel. The Spirit has ignited fires of grace in His churches and Christian communities throughout the world. The Spirit obviously wants the true church to embrace the true gospel of His grace. The church's part is to preach, teach, and demonstrate radical grace.

There is a caution in teaching radical grace. It may in certain cases be the instrument that causes division in some churches. Therefore the introduction of the grace message must be seasoned with love and understanding, to do otherwise is not grace. Our part as individuals is to teach grace by demonstrating it in our interactions with the church and the world. To do this we must ourselves maintain a steady diet of grace, and discipline ourselves to reject all teachings of law and/or mixtures.

This is not an easy task because we must show grace to those who believe differently and outright disagree with us. We should keep in mind that we had to be convinced of the simplicity of grace, and that false beliefs regarding a performance-based salvation were learned over a long period and we cannot dislodge them in just one effort.

Jesus calls the message of grace the, "Word of the kingdom." He likens this word to a seed that we must allow in our heart to produce its benefits in our lives. The hearers of the message of grace seem to fall into several groups. There are those that hear but for various reasons fail to understand and the devil steals the word from them. Then there are those who understand the message but they do not have any spiritual depth in their lives. They have no root system in the word of God so when things happen because of the grace message they become offended and abandon it. Then there are those that have knowledge of God's word and have applied it to a degree in their life. They hear and understand the message of grace but they have developed an undisciplined lifestyle and fail to do what is necessary to put grace into practice in their everyday activities. But many believe the message and pursue it with all their heart. They believe it and put it into practice in their lives, realizing that it is a continuing process. They take the seed of the message and allow it to become fruitful in their lives.

Lest there be a misunderstanding in the mind of the Christian that under grace sin can be taken lightly, forgiveness is an option, and Christian responsibility is relegated to a lackadaisical mind set, it must be emphatically emphasized that no place in the gospel of grace is this mindset even suggested as being true grace. Grace empowers us to walk in our righteous nature and never releases us to sin or downplays the seriousness of sin.

Although we are forgiven of all sin, and are not required to confess our sin to God, the serious Christian readily acknowledges his wrongdoings and solicits guidance from the Holy Spirit to progress past them. Forgiveness of others for their wrongs against us is not an option for the Christian. Unforgiveness harms both the offender and the one offended because it damages relationships that God desires. Throughout Paul's writings Christian responsibilities are stated. We do not accomplish these responsibilities to attain favor or righteousness but because of whom we are in Christ.

CHAPTER TWO

Divine Fellowship an Invitation to Dance

God has always purposed and planned to include all mankind in the loving relationship that exists within the Trinity. To believe otherwise is to have a distorted understanding of the love of God. Everything that exists has been birthed from the womb of the Holy Trinity and was designed and created with a divine purpose in the mind of God. Central to this purpose was the creation of a species called mankind that He designed in the image of the Trinity to be included in all the love and unity of the Trinity.

Beginning with His original creation of Adam and Eve, God revealed His heart for mankind as He extended and exercised this relationship with them in the garden. In the first mention of God in His record to mankind, God reveals Himself as Elohim. Elohim is the plural name for God. It identifies Him as a Trinity. The Scriptures reveal that this is the Trinity of perfect unity and fellowship, the optimum relationship that exists between the Father, Son, and Holy Spirit. Throughout the existence of mankind, God has extended this invitation of relationship and fellowship.

In the beginning, before there was a universe, before there was time, space, and matter, God existed in the persons of the Father, Son, and Holy Spirit. They existed in perfect union of essence, love, thought, and action. What was true of one was true of all. There was a perfect contentment and satisfaction within their unity. In his book, "Beyond an Angry God," Steve McVey has this to say about this relationship.

> "The Church Fathers uses a Greek word to describe this special relationship – *perichoresis*. The word first appears in writing in the seventh century and refers to what some have called a "community of being" in which each person of the Trinity, while maintaining His distinctive identity, shares His very essence with the others. The word denotes a oneness that creates a unified movement of intimate relationship – like a dance. Look again at the word *perichoresis*. It comes from the words *peri* and *chorein*. *Peri* denotes a circle, as in the word *perimeter*. *Chorein* means to make room for and to enclose. Dancing is a good metaphor for this loving, synchronized movement of the Father, Son, and Spirit enclosed together in one essence."

There came a point at which this Trinity decided to create a species of beings called mankind, and to include them in this relationship enjoyed by the Trinity. In preparation for the creation of mankind God spoke the universe into being and it began to expand at the speed of light. Within this universe God designed a minute but very significant planet called Earth on which He would place man. God anticipated everything that this man species would ever need and incorporated these into the original creation of this planet. Mankind was so designed that throughout his existence he would have an insatiable desire to search out and discover the remarkable nuggets that God had hidden within His original creation of planet Earth.

We only have to ponder all that mankind has discovered and developed throughout the years to realize that it was all there in the beginning. The discovery of electricity, sound waves, gravity, and all the wonders of science were all contained in the original design of God, for man's use. Man would need water, food, and a proper mixture of oxygen, so God made those a part of His creation as well as all else that man would need for his existence. God created a perfect world of land mass and water where He would place man to live. He then filled the earth with all manner of animal and plant life which He designed to reproduce after its kind. Each creation was so designed to be compatible with the environment in which He placed it. When all was prepared, God created man and placed him in this perfect environment. The desire for relationship and fellowship were part of God's original design for Adam and, therefore, mankind.

To partially satisfy this desire and provide a means for mankind to reproduce after its own kind, God took a rib from Adam and created him a helpmate to complement him. However, the level of relationship and fellowship desired by God can only be achieved through receiving the Trinity's invitation of salvation. Adam is the father of the human race; all mankind existed in him. When he fell, all mankind fell, thereby delaying God's desire to include them in the loving fellowship with the Trinity.

But God, in His predetermination to include all mankind, had a contingency plan. Since through Adam all mankind was infected with the sin principle the only solution, and freedom from this state, was for man to die. God's marvelous plan of recovery was consummated by sending His Son to be the representative to die for all mankind. When He died and was resurrected in their place He recovered all fallen mankind. His death and resurrection reconciled mankind to God from all the ramifications of sin.

Once again man was in a position to respond to the invitation of the Father to be included in fellowship with the Trinity. He was invited to take part in the dance. God does not desire that any of His creation perish but has left that choice to man. For whatever reasons exist in the minds and hearts of men for the rejection of this gracious offer of fellowship, God will not force His will upon them. Hell is a choice of man, not of God. That does not mean that God has ceased to love them and to extend to them every offer of grace.

In His construction of the Bible God reveals His efforts to reclaim, restore, and include man in a grace relationship where He loves with an unconditional love and desires to provide all that man needs for a life of abundance and favor. However, as recorded in history, most of mankind has always misunderstood and resisted this plan for relationship.

Throughout the history of mankind, God has maintained His tenacity to love all His creation. He has recorded specific Biblical events that allow us to see the extent that He was and is willing to go to offer this invitation to all.

With His divine choice of Abraham and his descendents, God presented a picture of how He desired to relate to man. He would at a later time allow Israel to choose how they wanted to relate to Him. This relationship is pictured in the contrast between the Old Covenant of law and the New Covenant of grace. One involves relying on one's ability to gain favor and love from God; the other involves receiving the favor and love of God simply because He chooses to give it, with no effort on the person's part. The covenant of grace was expressed in a limited manner through God's relationship with Abraham, and expressed in its fullest measure through the New Covenant extended to mankind as the culmination of the finished work of Jesus, the Son.

In choosing Abraham as a recipient of His grace, God reveals that this relationship is to be on an individual basis. With the inclusion of Abraham's descendents, the nation of Israel, God reveals that whole nations are to be included in this relationship; with the all-inclusive invitation of the New Covenant, God reveals that this relationship extends to all mankind.

Sadly, history also records how man has failed to respond to God's invitation of relationship. Abraham's descendents failed to take advantage of the covenant that God had made with Abraham, which included them. As a result they ended up as slaves in a heathen nation. God hears their cries of despair, remembered the covenant that still existed with them, called out Moses as their deliverer, and led them back into a place of dependency upon Him. He desired to re-establish them in a nation that He describes as flowing with milk and honey, where He alone would be their source for all things. After having experienced the miracles that freed them from the Egyptians and God's supernatural provisions for them while in the wilderness, they mistrusted Him and balked at His plan for establishing them in a nation of their own.

God's plan for them was delayed for forty years because of their stubborn refusal to trust Him. They insisted that they could maintain a relationship with Him through a different covenant than the one which was still in effect through Abraham, a covenant which required them to labor for everything that God had desired to provide them under their previous covenant.

Delivering them from their wilderness wanderings, God relocated them in the land He had promised, still desiring to be their God, and them to be His people. Once again He cultivated an opportunity for a divine relationship with them as a nation. Their response was to habitually reject this relationship, and His love and affection for them, even after God had demonstrated His ability to provide for them and cause them to triumph over their enemies. They also failed to be the example to other nations of what a nation could be like that totally trusted and depended upon God.

During this period all manner of heathen religious rites and rituals existed around Israel but Israel failed to provide a clear definitive picture of the love and character of God that would have enticed others to believe in their God. Although God made effort after effort though His prophets and priests to establish this loving relationship it was to no avail and this period of history closed with a four-hundred-year silence from God.

Jesus ushered in the Kingdom and a new era. He expressed to a sinful world the true picture of a loving Father, a loving Father who extends a divine invitation for all peoples to enter into a relationship with the Trinity and enjoy all the completeness that exists with the Father, Son, and Holy Spirit. This invitation of relationship, fellowship, love, favor, and provision is extended through the New Covenant initiated by God the Father through the finished work of the Son on the cross.

From the cross, when Jesus declared it was finished, He was terminating the old way of man relating to God and providing a plan whereby all men could be included in a divine relationship with the Father. He declared a plan where men were delivered from the old Adam and translated out of the darkness and into the light of the Kingdom of the dear Son. They could now relate to God from this new position, having died and arisen with Him. Since Christ died for all, then all died. He died for all so that those who live should live no longer for themselves, but for Him who died for them and rose again. Having done this, He placed all mankind in position to experience and enjoy an eternal relationship with God (II Corinthians 5:14-15).

The Holy Spirit assumes the responsibility to make every individual aware of this marvelous fact, that all have been reconciled and are loved by the Father. Although God provides both the faith and grace to enter into this divine relationship, He leaves the choice of that relationship to man. While God uses men and women to proclaim this gospel of grace and assigns to them the ministry of reconciliation, He takes full responsibility for penetrating the hearts of man with the truths of his love and acceptance. Only the Holy Spirit can do this.

The Old Covenant relationship ends with the death, burial, and resurrection of Jesus around the year of 33 A.D. The Old Covenant was made obsolete and terminated but from that time, until the destruction of the temple by Titus in 70 A.D., there was a transition period between the Old Covenant and the New Covenant. Evidence of this transition is recorded in the book of Hebrews and the writings of Paul. Paul's ministry was to present this new gospel of grace and the introduction of the New Covenant.

Paul was plagued by zealots of the Old Covenant who insisted that Paul's converts adhere to the requirements of the Old Covenant. Paul was adamant that this was not true and insisted that it was Jesus plus nothing. With the destruction of the temple in 70 A.D., Titus not only destroyed the hub for the Old Covenant worship and caused the people to be scattered throughout the world, he also destroyed them as a nation. They did not become a nation again until 1948. Coming together again as the nation Israel, they continued with many of the Old Covenant's requirements but terminated animal sacrifice. They continue, as do many of the New Covenant Christians, to relate to God through efforts of worship and self-performance outlined under the Old Covenant.

Even though God has reconciled all men unto Himself, under the canopy of the New Covenant, not all is well. Men have persisted in, and still persist in, defining their relationship to God and others through various self-effort means. These run a broad spectrum from individual interpretation and application of the Holy Scriptures to the total rejection of all divine guidance. The results have left the world in a chaotic state where men largely live by a creed of doing whatever is right in their own eyes.

Within the scope of the gospel of grace- or to be more precise, often the absence thereof- there exists division rather than the unity that is clearly spelled out under the provision of the New Covenant. There is a gross lack of teaching and demonstration of the gospel of grace by a great many Christian churches. This void has been infiltrated with a large infection of religious beliefs that have no foundation in the Scriptures. Within the scope of Christianity men persist in incorporating a mixture of the requirements of the Old Covenant with the freedoms of the New Covenant. This has lead to a doctrine that embraces being saved by grace but regulates all manner of things that one must do to be approved.

Christian cloning is the concept of cookie-cutter sheep where all embrace a set of doctrinal beliefs to the absence of the teaching that each person must individually hear the Holy Spirit (Matthew 4:4). Many of these doctrines do include the wonderful Biblical beliefs that have provided understanding and comfort to large numbers of Christians. I do not in any manner fault these. Where I do take issue, however, is with those mixing the covenants and promoting self-effort performances that rob Christians of their freedom and hinder the relationship that God desires with them. I must hasten to say that I believe all Christian churches desire and intend to follow the teachings of God and provide their parishioners with guidelines that help them navigate the difficulties of life. I just believe that many misinterpretations and misapplications of Scriptures have caused a deviation from what God actually intended to what is actually practiced. It is in this gap that error abounds and building on sand takes place.

Grace is the only ingredient that will bring solidarity to the Church and make it the lighthouse for the world. Under the tent of Christianity there exist many conflicting and contradicting doctrines and beliefs. One must wonder how the world sees us when we identify ourselves as Methodist, Baptist, Lutheran, Episcopalian, Catholic, Pentecostal, Charismatic, Evangelical, fundamentalist, and on and on, and present ourselves to the lost world as "Christians." This is not to downplay the importance of each of these individual denominations but it must foster confusion to the outsider; they must wonder, "Can all with different doctrines and beliefs be right?" Most major heathen religions present more solidarity within their own bodies than does Christianity. Examine Buddhism, Confucianism, Hinduism, and Islam. Grace, as Paul taught it, is the only answer to create solidarity among so many diverse congregations.

In the midst of the confusion and misunderstanding between the peoples of God as to what is required of them to be accepted by Him, and of a world that has alienated itself from Him, God still persists in having that loving relationship with all those He has reconciled. He has initiated a recurrence of a pure, radical gospel of grace that is invading the spheres of His people: a grace that has as its essence the totally unconditional love of God; a grace that declares that it has all been done, it is finished, God has met and exceeded all the requirements for men to enjoy a relationship with Him; a grace that frees from having to perform in order to be righteous to a grace that empowers us to perform because we are already righteous; a grace that provides us with the love of God so that we can love as He does; a grace that declares all the promises of God are "yes!"; a grace that not only provides life but provides an abundant life where everything that is needed for life and godliness is available; a grace that is always the gospel, good news and never bad news; and a grace that includes mankind in the oneness and fellowship of the Holy Trinity. Bottom line, it is the gospel of grace alone that can unify and empower the church to take the message of reconciliation to the unbelieving world.

Chapter Three

New Covenant Righteousness

One of the governing desires of most Christians is to consistently maintain a life of perceived righteousness (right doing, right standing) in their relationship with God and with others. In an attempt of how to successfully accomplish this, Christians organizations, as well as local congregations, have developed teachings, steps, and different rules of conduct to assist the individual Christian in doing what is considered right. Much ministerial counseling involves instructing individuals with problems on how to apply these rules to their specific situation. This may vary from local congregation to local congregation but the basis for this teaching involves what an individual must do in order to be included within the realms of accepted righteousness. The motivation for these teachings is to be commended but the application often fosters a work-out-your-own-righteousness mentality.

Christians respond to life situations governed by the paradigms they have developed in their lives. These paradigms are developed from acceptable social behavior as well as from what they have been taught and their personal interpretation of the Scriptures. Largely these beliefs adopt the mindset that for one to be righteous he must perform righteous acts and maintain righteous attitudes.

To validate these rules of conduct appropriate, Scripture verses are selected that describe righteous acts and attitudes that must be performed. For instance one is to be kind, merciful, loving, forgiving, generous, and the list goes on and on. The motivation for extending these Christian gracelets determines whether we believe we must do them to be righteous or because we are righteous.

While this stress on the performance of righteous deeds as proof of our righteousness certainly appears to the serious Christian as a valid teaching, the root of this theology is based upon a false concept that righteousness is something that one must do rather than what one is through the new birth. Righteousness can be defined as "right standing before God." This is only made possible through the finished work of Jesus and is a once-for-all event. Righteous is not something that we must do; it is something that God has made us through the new birth. We are encouraged to "rightly divide the word of truth." Because when we develop our theology around a false understanding or application of a scriptural concept, we forfeit the, "You shall know the truth and the truth shall set you free," benefit of that intended scriptural concept.

When our beliefs and applications of a Scripture place us in bondage rather than liberating us, we have a false understanding of that Scripture or its application to us under the New Covenant. Jesus has liberated us from the laws of performance and provided for us a more excellent way. To constantly live under the weight of having to perform certainly is not a more excellent way. When a person lives under the constant pressure of having to evaluate his performance as the measure of his righteousness, the result leads to a sin consciousness rather than a righteousness consciousness. God's grace has eliminated this requirement by making us the righteousness of God in Christ Jesus. Hallelujah!

Paul addresses the two taught methods of attaining righteousness in Romans Chapter Ten.

Romans 10:1 – Brethren, my hearts' desire and prayer to God for Israel is that they may be saved.

- Paul had experienced the liberty from having to accomplish all the requirements of the Old Covenant laws and earnestly desired that his fellow Israelites experience the same freedom. He states this as the message for all Christians in II Corinthians 5:18-19.

Romans 10:2 – For I bear them witness that they have a zeal for God, but not according to knowledge.

- Paul, a Pharisee of Pharisees, would know something about misguided zeal for righteousness through one's efforts. The sad indictment is that many in the modern church have fallen victim to this work-out-your-own salvation mentality due to a lack of knowledge regarding the Scriptures about the grace of God. Those that pursue righteousness through their own efforts have a zeal to please God but they are just misguided in their methods to do so.

Romans 10:3 – For they being ignorant of God's righteousness, and seeking to establish their own righteousness, have not submitted to the righteousness of God.

- This identifies the root cause of why most churches teach some type of performance to attain or maintain righteousness. It is based upon a false concept of what is the meaning of righteousness. From man's perception righteousness is what he is required to do for God, while the righteousness of God rests entirely upon what Christ has already done for us.

- II Corinthians 5:21 – For He made Him who knew no sin to be sin for us, that we might become the righteousness of God in Him.

- Righteousness is not a state to be achieved; it is a provision that places a person in right standing before a holy God regardless of his performance.

- God creates us as righteous beings. We have His DNA. This is a birthright, not an act to be performed. We do not "do to be"; we do because we be.

Romans 10:4 – For Christ is the end of the law for righteousness to everyone who believes.
- This is a declaration that we are free from the law of performance when we believe in Christ. There is only one way for a person to become righteous, he must be born again. It is not possible for a person to attain righteousness by following the laws of the Old Covenant, nor by following the performances established by modern-day Christian groups.

Romans 10:5 – For Moses writes about the righteousness which is of the law, "The man who does those things shall live by them."
- Paul quotes from Leviticus 18:5 that requires one to live by the dictates of the law to maintain a relationship with God. However, through the finished work of Jesus Christ this changed from what a man must do to what Jesus had done.
- In Galatians 5:3 Paul emphatically declares when one has believed in Christ and becomes joint heirs with Him, and then goes back under the law, this person has fallen from the benefits provided by the grace of God.

- Galatians 5:1-4 clearly define what Paul means. To attempt to follow even one of the old laws the person is required to follow all 613 laws. The person attempting to live by any means of performance to please God is in fact declaring that the finished work of Jesus was not enough and forfeits the benefits of this finished work in his life.
- In Chapter three of Galatians Paul calls them foolish to try and achieve spiritual maturity though acts of the flesh rather than continuing in the Spirit.

Romans 10:6 – But the righteousness of faith speaks in this way, "Do not say in your heart, 'Who will ascend into heaven?'" (that is, to bring Christ down from above),

Romans 10:7 – or, "'Who will descend into the abyss?'" (that is, to bring Christ up from the death).
- At this time Jesus had already died and risen and ascended to the right hand of God. He had finished all that was required for mankind to be reconciled with God. Paul is using an Old Testament Scripture to say that this righteousness by faith is not difficult to understand. You don't have to have someone come explain it to you.

Romans 10:8 – But what does it say? "The word is near you, in your mouth and in your heart," (that is, the word of faith, which we preach).
- How could Paul say that the word of God was in the heart and mouth of a person, even a lost person? We start by understanding the meaning of the "word" used here. In the Greek there are two words that are translated into English as "word." The first is "Logos" which includes the complete word of God. In John 1:1 Jesus is identified as the "Logos" of God.
- The second word is "Rhema" which means the specific word of God, the revelation that the Holy Spirit gives a person regarding a particular verse or portion of Scripture or any life issue. Rhema is the word used in this verse.

- Rhema also includes revelations that the Holy Spirit gives us as guidance and understanding in life activities. Jesus states in Matthew 4:4 that man shall live by every word (Rhema) that proceeds from the mouth of God. These personal words may not be a quote from Scripture but the thoughts and words the Holy Spirit gives to guide us in maturing into the person that God says we are and in attaining all that He says we can do.
- Next, in Titus 2:11 Paul writes that the grace of God that brings salvation has appeared to <u>all men</u>. The open invitation to salvation is extended to every person by the Holy Spirit. This grace would certainly have enlightened the heart of those to whom it appeared. Again, Paul says this invitation has appeared to all mankind.
- John 1:9 –That was the true Light which gives light to <u>every man</u> coming into the world. Jesus came to provide every person with the illumination to be included in redemption (I John 2:2).
- We are assured in Ephesians 2:8-9 that both the faith and grace required for our complete salvation is provided to us. It is the ministry of the Holy Spirit to provide us with the knowledge and faith for salvation and then release grace to make it happen.
- II Corinthians 4:6 – For it is the God who commanded light to shine out of darkness, who has shone in our hearts to give the light of the knowledge of the glory of God in the face of Jesus Christ.
- Romans 1:19 – Because what may be known of God is manifest <u>in them</u>, for God has shown it to them.
- Even those that choose to reject God are presented with the invitation to participate in salvation.
- II Corinthians 4:3-4 – But even if our gospel is veiled, it is veiled to those who are perishing whose minds the god of this age has blinded, who do not believe, lest the light of the gospel of the glory of Christ, who is the image of God, should shine on them.
- By these Scriptures we are assured that it is the Holy Spirit that puts this knowledge in our hearts that we may confess it with our mouths and receive the benefits of salvation. Although God

uses men to make the world aware of the love of God and His invitation for salvation, He does not trust the final results to the abilities of man. The conclusion is that God so loves mankind that He reveals the knowledge of Himself to them in such a way that they may believe and participate in His salvation.

- The Holy Spirit is not limited by the mental or physical condition of the person.

Romans 10:9 – That if you confess with your mouth the Lord Jesus, and believe in your heart that God has raised Him from the dead, you will be saved.

Romans 10:10 – For with the heart one believes unto righteousness, and with the mouth confession is made unto salvation.

- These verses describe a person's response to the revelation given them by the Holy Spirit. It is their response to the light that is shone in their hearts and makes them beneficiaries of God's salvation for them.
- Abraham believed God and it was accounted to him as righteousness. The individual believes God and is made the righteousness of God.

The Greek word for righteousness is "Dikaiosune." It is a noun and defines righteousness as being a divine righteousness of which God is the source. Although the church at large defines righteousness as a verb by assigning it various acts that one must perform to maintain a righteous relationship with God and others, the Scriptures identify righteousness as justification or right standing before God. While it is often taught that righteousness is acquired by following certain acts of conduct, the Scriptures reveal that righteousness is a gift from God and is acquired through faith in Him (Romans 5:17).

It should be a great relief for us to understand that righteousness by faith is not acquired by following religious rules; neither is it based upon our goodness. Just as a person does not become a sinner because he sins, he cannot become righteous by performing righteous acts. A person is a sinner because of his position in the first Adam. In the same manner, a person is righteous because of his position in the last Adam.

Perhaps you have said, or heard others say, "When God looks at me He does not see me but sees Jesus." What they are inferring is that if God were to see them as they really are He would be greatly disappointed. Nothing could be further from the truth. When God sees us, He sees each one as a new person that He has created. Our Father is the same as Jesus' Father; we are birthed by the same Holy Spirit that birthed Jesus. When God sees us, He sees a son or daughter that He has perfectly created. He sees us just as righteous as Jesus. It is a Biblical truth that we are in Jesus and Jesus is in the Father, therefore we are also in the Father. Each one's spirit does not look any different than God's Spirit.

In conclusion, righteousness is something we are, not something we do. We are righteous regardless of how we feel or how we act. We are righteous because we are God's creation and He does not create unrighteousness. Because we are righteous we perform righteous acts and develop righteous attitudes and lifestyles through the grace provided by the Holy Spirit.

Learning to believe, develop, and live as the righteous person He has made us is a lifelong process. It involves developing an identity based upon who God says we are and renewing our minds to think as He thinks. It requires a constant changing of our paradigms to align with the revelations that He gives us. A major factor in walking in righteousness is our desire to listen and follow the voice of God in our lives. Man lives righteously by every word that proceeds from the mouth of God.

To appreciate and understand God's righteous relationship with people, it is important to understand the means by which He relates to them. The Kingdom of God is the realm through which God relates to mankind and all that He does in His Kingdom is righteous. God's righteous love is the motivating force that guides all His activities with people. God's goodness is the manifestation of His love throughout His Kingdom. God has established an unbreakable covenant with His Son. He has expressed His desire that all mankind participate with His Son in this covenant. The Holy Spirit delivers invitations to all mankind and provides the faith and grace to respond. This is called the gospel. To participate in this covenant all one must do is utilize the faith provided and believe in the gospel (good news) of grace.

CHAPTER FOUR

Repentance - the Renewing of the Mind

Many Western churches, in an attempt to provide guidance for their members on the "how tos" of a holy life, stress the importance of repentance. There is indeed a genuine need to stress the importance of New Covenant repentance. However, in most cases the church has wrongly adopted the Webster dictionary definition of repentance that involves the remorse and turning from sinful acts in one's life. Honesty will concede we categorize our sins from socially acceptable sins to those on the far end of the spectrum of what are identified as gross sins against God and man. In doing so we tend to acclimate ourselves to excusing certain sins while feeling remorse for only the greater violations.

To assist individual members in how to deal with personal sin, the church in many cases has developed a doctrinal concept of how to manage these sins. This concept, whether written or unwritten, involves the repentance of sins by confessing these sins and then ceasing from doing them. Under this process the individual must develop a continuous awareness of sin in his everyday life. He then must express the proper measure of remorse, depending upon the magnitude of the sin, regarding this failure to measure up. Needless to say this leads the individual to develop a lifestyle of sin consciousness that requires a constant self-examination.

As well meaning as this procedure is, it offers little help in changing the individual's inclination to sin. The simple fact is the individual is attempting to change himself by focusing on what Jesus died to free him from. If confessing and feeling bad regarding sin had been the solution, then Jesus need not to have died for the solution to sin was within the individual.

Because much of the church maintains that we are just sinners saved by grace it has led to a sin consciousness rather than making members aware of the Biblical fact that they are indeed the righteousness of God, the handiwork of God Himself. By focusing on sin both from the pulpit and in individual situations the church has actually strengthened the desire to sin in the individual.

The Bible states that the strength of sin is the law (I Corinthians 15:56). Simply put this means that where there is a law prohibiting something, the flesh will justify violating that law when the occasion arises. Traffic speed laws are an example. The focus then shifts to not violating the law rather than embracing our true identity in Christ that only desires to demonstrate the righteous characteristics of the Kingdom of God. The focus is on what the individual must not do rather than focus on who he is in Christ Jesus. The problem here is that it causes the person to focus on something that God declares He has forgiven and forgotten. To try to focus on righteousness and sin at the same time is double-mindedness. It is spiritual schizophrenia.

To apply this type of repentance a person must first of all have a complete knowledge of the true definition of sins, not just what man identifies as sins. Secondly, he must have complete comprehension of every sin that he commits during the period of his confession and not categorize them into small, medium, and large sins.

Human emotions are fickle and can be manipulated depending upon the situation and are poor indicators of true change in one's behavior. Many examples can be cited. A drunkard may truly feel remorse for things that he does while drunk and even vow to change, but still continue to repeat them. Personal habits that lead one to sin may afterward cause the individual to have deep remorse for his weakness but that does not solve his problem and free him from the habit. True repentance addresses the root of the problem rather than the fruit of the problem.

The process of renewing the mind is the first step to true repentance because it causes a person to change the paradigms in their lives and in doing so change their actions. A paradigm is a set of acquired beliefs that govern everything about us, how we make decisions, how we relate to others, how we dress, what we believe about ourselves and others, and on which we base our security of salvation. They are the compasses that guide us through life activities.

True repentance, changing the mind, involves more than just voicing one's confession that he now holds a different belief than he previously held regarding a Biblical matter. True repentance involves embracing a Biblical truth and making that truth part of one's paradigm.

An example of true repentance is to believe that Jesus died for every sin, past, present, and future. Therefore the need to confess sins in order to be forgiven is not a Biblical truth. This will free the person to live a life that is not sin conscious but righteous conscious.

Understanding how Jesus viewed repentance will foster a greater revelation of how we should apply repentance in our daily lives. Now after John was put in prison, Jesus came to Galilee preaching the "gospel" of the Kingdom of God, and saying, "The time is fulfilled, and the Kingdom of God is at hand. Repent and believe in the "gospel," (Mark 1:14-15, emphasis mine). Then Paul said, "John indeed baptized with a baptism of repentance, saying to the people that they should believe on Him who would come after him, that is, on Christ Jesus," (Acts_19:4, emphasis mine).

To appreciate true Biblical repentance it is necessary to understand what Jesus meant when He said "repent." It is apparent from the Scripture in Mark that repentance is associated with believing the "good news" of the Kingdom of God, which Paul stresses is belief in Jesus.

To aid us in understanding what Jesus meant it is helpful to understand the mindset of the people in Jesus' time. The nation of Israel was birthed as a miracle. Abraham and Sarah had a miracle child, Isaac, when they were past the child-bearing age of life. From this son were born twins, Esau and Jacob. Jacob had twelve sons who eventually became the nation of Israel. Because of unbelief the descendants of Abraham abandoned their covenant promises and as a result ended up for four hundred years in bondage in Egypt. During these four hundred years there was no guidance from God. In their bondage they cried out.

God heard their cry and remembered His covenant with them and, through a series of miracles by Moses, freed them from their taskmasters and led them to a land that was to be theirs where He would be their God. After leaving Egypt they arrived at Mt. Sinai where rather than renewing the promises of their existing covenant with God, they instead entered into a different covenant with Him that required them to obey numerous laws and statutes. In order for them to have their sins forgiven and remain in a right relationship with God they must constantly be aware of these strict requirements and obey these laws.

This constant pressure of keeping all these laws was the prevailing lifestyle of Israel until the coming of Jesus. This was ingrained into the mind and life of every Israelite. This was their paradigm, their belief system that governed their lifestyle. With the giving of the law on Mt. Sinai the lifestyle of the children of Israel changed drastically. From the lifestyle of grace offered to them under the Abrahamic covenant (which contained no punishments), theirs lives were now governed by 613 laws that contained punishments and were impossible to keep. Their paradigms were based entirely upon how well they could maintain life activities under these laws.

During the years after entering the land promised by God they continued in this type of lifestyle. The history of their journey from Mt. Sinai until the prophet Malachi reveals that they were constant violators of this covenant of laws. As a result they were taken into bondage to other nations and scattered throughout the world. After the prophet Malachi, God ceased to speak and guide them as He had previously done through prophets and priests for a period of <u>four hundred years</u>. This seems to exactly parallel what had happened to these same descendants of Abraham when they ended up in bondage down in Egypt for <u>four hundred years</u>.

After four hundred years and not hearing from a prophet, John the Baptist came preparing the way for Jesus by preaching a message of repentance. Jesus was baptized by John, anointed by the Holy Spirit, and began His ministry. After John was put in prison, Jesus came preaching a message of good news about a new kingdom.

He addresses their ingrained mindset developed under the Old Covenant and tells them to change their mind to believe this new gospel. They understood the repentance that John preached for the remission of sin, but with this new gospel of the Kingdom, Jesus came preaching not repentance from sin, but a repentance to the good news He was preaching. Through repentance He offers them deliverance from the bondage of their current lifestyle. Grace and truth came through Jesus.

With the good news of the kingdom, Jesus tells them to repent, change their way of thinking, and believe this new gospel (this new way of relating to God) and having their sins forgiven. It is clear that what Jesus was saying to them was to stop believing in their old paradigm (their old way of relating to God) and establish a new paradigm based upon the good news of the Kingdom of God. Jesus preached for about three years. One must conclude that during that time He preached many sermons and it would be inconceivable to think that He did not thoroughly explain what the good news of the Kingdom was.

The New Testament Greek word for repentance is "Metanoeo" which means to change the mind, to change the inner man. The idea expressed in the Greek is that if one changes the way they believe, changes their paradigm, it will cause them to change the way they act. It is to be understood that this is progressive throughout our lives. If we truly want to embrace the truths of the Kingdom we will be constantly repenting and adjusting our beliefs to align with those truths. It is impossible for a person to believe that they are just a dirty sinner, yet experience victory in their lives consistently.

Just a casual study of New Testament Scriptures will reveal that it is the Greek definition and not the definition that the church has attached to "repentance" that Jesus is referring to. Beginning with the fact that Jesus died to secure for us the forgiveness for all our sins, it must follow that since we are forever forgiven for all sins, and God does not remember them anymore, that He does not now condemn or punish us for sin. Then, this repentance must be something different. Why would God want us to grieve and feel sorry for the very sin that He has already forgiven and forgotten?

It is clear then that Jesus was saying that in order for us to receive the benefits of grace provided in the Kingdom we must change our thinking and believing to agree with His teachings of the gospel of the Kingdom of God. In Christ we are a new creation; we must adjust our belief system to think as a new creation.

The New Testament Epistles stress the responsibilities and character qualities that are expected and desired of a Christian. A person is enabled to fulfill these responsibilities as he renews his mind to align with the gospel of grace. Paul states that the mind must be renewed in order to discern the intent of the will of God (Romans 12:2).

Although I have little scientific knowledge of how the human brain functions, I offer the following thoughts not as scientific fact, but as an attempt to put in layman terms how the function of the brain relates to repentance. I believe that even this shallow understanding of the brain's activity will assist us in grasping the Biblical function of renewing the mind.

The ingenuity of the human brain is clearly evidence of the creativity of God. It is more sophisticated than all the man-made computers together. It is constantly recording, cataloging, and storing data. It receives this data through the five gates of our senses, i.e., sight, hearing, taste, touch, and smell. The brain then stores this data in each of these compartments with at least two additional compartments, the mind and the emotions.

Because of the knowledge stored in each of these departments we easily identify certain sights, sounds, tastes, and smells that are common in our world because we have been exposed to them and they are recorded in our brain. Similarly we can identify certain objects by touch. The mind is filled with the knowledge to recall and define facts learned years ago and use these facts in current situations. In addition, we are constantly expressing a wide variety of emotions as we interact with the world around us. Emotions may be good or bad, an asset or a liability depending on the response. This can be evidenced by what causes our emotions to trigger our sympathetic nervous system in its fight or flight responses. They may be real or imagined.

The brain uses the information stored in these different compartments to formulate our decisions, responses, and reactions to life activities and situations. When we encounter a situation the brain analyzes the situation based upon stored data. For example, you are walking through a wooded area and hear a rattling sound. Your brain instantly analyzes from its data that the sound is associated with a rattlesnake. The brain then dictates which action to take, stand very still or jump and run. This gathering of stored data is what forms the paradigms of our lives. It is from this source that we make the decisions that determine who we believe ourselves to be and how we facilitate life matters.

The brain is constantly upgrading these compartments with newly learned facts/information. Because much of the stored knowledge comes from world sources it may be partially true or altogether false. The brain is constantly upgrading its information to reflect the newer data. This applies to all the compartments. One may have been taught something they believed to be true and this belief influenced their decisions. When they learn new data that shows the first to be false the old data is replaced with this new data/knowledge/information. As the data changes so does the individual's paradigm. As the paradigm changes so does the actions of the individual regarding the new data. Understanding this simple but complex process will help us understand how the Biblical renewing of the mind must be accomplished. The procedure is simple but the process becomes very complex beyond explanation because of the innumerable results it provides.

There are certain key verses of Scripture that highlight a dynamic spiritual principle necessary for a Christian to experience a productive life in the Kingdom of God. Although the importance of these Scriptures can be easily understood, the mechanics of accomplishing and attaining the results of these Scriptures can only be achieved through the understanding and application of other meaningful Scriptures. The following are a few such examples.

II Timothy 2:15 – Be diligent to present yourself approved to God, a worker who does not need to be ashamed, rightly dividing the word of truth.

- The dangers of not rightly dividing the word of truth, the Scriptures, are readily realized when we observe the misinterpretation and misapplication exercised by the various Christian bodies. Just a shallow study of the differences that exists in the doctrines of the major evangelical bodies will verify they all do not use the same method of interpretation of the Scriptures. This has been the cause of great damage and division among God's people.

- The misapplication of I John 1:9 alone has led many modern churches to adopt an unbiblical doctrine that places literally millions of Christians in bondage. This misapplication requires the Christian to constantly confess sins the Bible clearly teaches God has already forgiven and forgotten.
- When this Scripture is examined in the light of the New Covenant the conclusion will be that it obviously applies to a person who is not a believer.
- Although the importance of rightly dividing the word of truth is readily apparent the "how to" accomplish this is not stated in this verse.

II Peter 3:18 – But grow in the grace and knowledge of our Lord and Savior Jesus Christ. To Him be the glory both now and forever. Amen.

- Throughout this book, Peter refers to "knowledge." Although the English language does not reveal the difference in the types of knowledge that Peter refers to, the Greek rendering is very precise.
- The Greek uses two different words for the different types of knowledge. The Greek word "Gnosis" refers to a general gathering of different types of knowledge—a knowledge acquired from first-hand experience. It is only as good as its source. It may be abstract or general knowledge. This could be referred to as "head knowledge."
- The second Greek word for knowledge is "Epignosis." This refers to a greater gathering of specific areas of information that leads to a fuller understanding of specific areas of knowledge. It includes knowledge received through divine revelation. This type of knowledge includes a personal embracing and application of the specific knowledge, and can be referred to as "experiential knowledge."
- A person may attend schools for several years gaining knowledge to become a surgeon. This knowledge could be a combination of Gnosis and Epignosis; however, it does

not become experiential knowledge until he has operated on someone.

- This verse states the desire of every serious Christian to grow in grace and knowledge but does not give instructions on how to accomplish it.

Romans 12:2 – And do not be conformed to this world, but be transformed by the renewing of your mind, that you may prove what is that good and acceptable and perfect will of God.

- In their eagerness to reach the masses some churches have compromised their spiritual integrity by adopting (conforming to) methods from the world system. This has diminished the clear differences that should exist between the church and the world.
- The purpose for renewing the mind is clearly outlined in this verse but there are no instructions on how a person must do this. Many helpful suggestions and methods have been offered to help one accomplish this, but most have had little effect in renewing the mind.

John 8:31-32 – Then Jesus said to those Jews who believed Him, "If you abide in My word, you are My disciples indeed. And you shall know the truth and the truth shall make you free."
- These verses state a very important truth relevant to the serious followers of Jesus. They are to constantly live their lives according to His word. This necessitates actively studying His word and applying it in their lives. His promise to them is that these truths will set them free. Obviously the truth He refers to here is the truths associated with the gospel of the Kingdom.
- It is evident from these verses that the truths which set one free must address those areas and issues that hold one in bondage. However, these verses do not outline guidelines of how to abide in His word nor do they furnish us with the means of discerning the truths that will set us free.

Matthew 4:4 – But He answered and said, "It is written, 'Man shall not live by bread alone, but by every word that proceeds from the mouth of God.'"

- Every sincere Christian realizes that everything God says is important. However, the underlying truth that Jesus presents here is that for a person to live by every word that proceeds from the mouth of God, he must actively listen and hear God speak.
- Since the individual is to live by what God says, what God says must apply to the individual, and if it applies to the individual, and is needed to live by, it must include those things that are relevant to that individual's life.
- Since it is a life matter to live by what God says, then what He says must provide guidance in all areas of the person's life.
- The words that God speaks are both spiritual and life.

John 16:13 – However, when He, the Spirit of truth, has come, He will guide you into all truth, for He will not speak on His own authority but whatever He hears He will speak; and He will tell you things to come.

- First, the Holy Spirit is the only One in all of Scripture who is identified as the One who can lead us into all truth. This is one of His primary ministries.
- Second, this Scripture implies that a person must develop a lifestyle of listening to the Holy Spirit for guidance in all areas of his life.
- We are given both the assurance and comfort that the Holy Spirit will lead us into all truth and will provide guidance for our future.

It is only when we combine all these Scriptures together that we get a much clearer picture of the principles intended in the individual Scriptures. We are also provided with the mechanics of how each individual directive of each Scripture is accomplished.

To be able to rightly divide the word of truth and grow in grace and the knowledge of God a person must have a personal relationship with God and desire God's guidance in every area of his life. It is understood that to receive this guidance one must have an active time of listening to God.

We understand from these Scriptures that the person of the Godhead that provides this guidance and these truths is the Holy Spirit. The Holy Spirit gives us the same interpretation and application of the Scriptures as God intended them (II Corinthians 2:10). When the Holy Spirit reveals these truths to us and we receive them and apply them in our lives we are set free from being conformed to this world and false interpretation of the Scriptures. This is the true Christian life and is abiding in His word.

This process is the genuine renewing of the mind because it replaces our thoughts, beliefs, and paradigms with the things of God. Since this process produces inner change it results in a change of our outward behavior and can be referred to as "growing in grace and the knowledge of God." This is what Jesus meant when He declared, "Repent and believe in the gospel." Repentance is a constant renewing of the mind to believing the good news of the Kingdom.

To expound further on the important subject of repentance is not meant to be redundant but to offer additional thoughts of clarification. As stated, the first step to true New Testament repentance involves the renewing of the mind. This renewing process involves understanding, believing, and acting upon the Scriptures as God meant them. Critical to this process is the revelation of the Scriptures that is freely given by the Holy Spirit. Without the enlightening of the Scriptures by the Holy Spirit man will continue to form his own Interpretations, leading to failures and confusions in his life.

Jesus provided us with very clear instructions on how this is to be done and the results it would produce. He said that man should live by every word that proceeds from the mouth of God (Matt. 4:4). He also said that if we abide in His word that we shall know the truth and the truth would set us free (John 8:31-32). It is the combination of these two truths that guarantees the Christian can have an abundant life.

The Greek rendering for "word" here refers to those personal truths of instructions, guidance, encouragement, and comfort that God speaks to the individual. The Holy Spirit enlightens these words so that the individual can understand their meaning and application. This is the same method that the Holy Spirit uses when giving us revelation regarding the Scriptures. When the individual receives the word and acts upon it the word produces the results promised. This becomes an experiential knowledge in the individual that frees him from areas of unbiblical thinking.

From a casual understanding of the function of our brain we realize that our lives are greatly governed by the information that is stored in the compartments of our brain. To change our actions and thoughts we must replace this information with new knowledge. We replace the learned information of the world with the spiritual knowledge about God and the good news of His grace; the Holy Spirit uses this knowledge to tutor us into being all that God says we are, and He empowers us to accomplish all that is required of us as one of His children. Jesus declares this to be essential for understanding and leading a productive life in the Kingdom of God. Timothy refers to this as rightly dividing the word of truth.

The following are some supporting Scriptures for Biblical repentance. Some are repeated for fuller understanding.

Philippians 2:5 – Let this mind be in you that was also in Christ Jesus.
- Paul tells us in I Corinthians 2:16 that we have the mind of Christ. The focus here is to allow His thoughts to be our thoughts, to learn to think as He does.

- Philippians 4:8 – Provides guidelines for maintaining the mind of Christ.

Matthew 11:29 – Take My yoke upon you and learn from Me, for I am gentle and lowly in heart, and you will find rest for your souls.
- This is a metaphor encouraging us to allow Jesus to lead us. He desires for us to learn of Him, from Him.

Romans 12:2 – And do not be conformed to this world, but be transformed by the renewing of your mind, that you may prove what is that good and acceptable and perfect will of God.
- Do not be molded by the world system
- Do not allow worldly paradigms to be the compass for your life.
- The word "transformed" is transfigured. It is the same word used in Matthew 17:2 – where Jesus was transfigured. He was transfigured from the inside out.
- This transformation comes by renewing the mind, thinking that aligns with the grace gospel.
- Although this transformation first takes place internally it will obviously manifest itself externally.
- Benefit of this transformation is to know the good, acceptable, and perfect will of God (regarding His kingdom and the New Covenant).

Philippians 4:8 – Finally, brethren, whatever things are <u>true</u>, whatever things are <u>noble</u>, whatever things are <u>just</u>, whatever things are <u>pure</u>, whatever things are <u>lovely</u>, whatever things are of <u>good report</u>, if there is any virtue and if there is anything praiseworthy – <u>meditate on these things.</u>
- These verses give us insight in how to maintain the mind of Christ.
- They give us insight in how to recognize unproductive thoughts.
- We are to meditate on the meaning and value of these things. Because they help us attain moral excellence (virtue).
- These are excellent guidelines for forming our paradigms.

Romans 8: 5 – For those who live according to the flesh set their minds on the things of the flesh, but those who live according to the Spirit, the things of the Spirit.

Romans 8:6 – For to be carnally minded is death, but to be spiritually minded is life and peace.

Romans 8:7 – Because the carnal mind is enmity against God; for it is not subject to the law of God, nor indeed can be. (1John 3:23, Hebrews 8:10)

Romans 10: 9 -10 – That if you confess with your mouth the Lord Jesus and believe in your heart that God has raised Him from the dead, you will be saved, for with the heart one believes unto righteousness, and with the mouth confession is made unto salvation.

The emphasis of these verses is that it is the belief that originates in the heart that governs what we think and do. It is a renewing of the mind that comes from the inner man. It is not just a shallow mental assent but one that is birthed by the illuminating of the Holy Spirit from the heart. There is a desperate need in the church to repent, renew our minds, and believe that the gospel of grace is true and adjust our lives to those truths.

Chapter Five

Spiritual Warfare

The picture that many Christians have regarding spiritual warfare is one of a person dressed in the spiritual armor of a knight going into battle against the spiritual enemies of the individual, family, and Kingdom of God. The picture is one of attacking the devil and his cohorts to prevent them from harming, harassing, killing, destroying, and plundering individuals, families, and churches.

This picture is much like a David and Goliath confrontation. It includes storming satanic strongholds to defeat the enemy and thus freeing individuals, cities, and nations to have peace from demonic activity. This type of spiritual warfare involves binding the activities of demons, loosing those under demonic influence, anointing portals, pulpits and pews, commanding demons to respond in various ways (i.e. go to the pit), and restricting demonic activities. I am afraid that much of this activity is similar to Don Quixote and his windmills. Although the motivation for this warfare is commendable, much of what transpires as spiritual warfare has no scriptural support because it fails to take into account the finished work of Jesus.

I John 3:8- He who sins is of the devil, for the devil has sinned from the beginning. For this purpose the Son of God was manifested, that <u>He might destroy the works of the devil.</u>

- Here John lays the source of all sin at the feet of the devil. Since the devil sinned from the beginning, and instigated the sin of Adam and Eve in the garden, all who sin participate to some degree in the spirit that initiated the very first sin. Therefore all sin directly or indirectly can be attributed to the devil. It is obvious that this verse does not mean that everyone who sins is a child of the devil. Christians are birthed by God and have a divine nature and yet they are still capable of performing sinful acts, but that does not make them a child of the devil. It simply means when one sins he is doing as the devil would do in that situation.

We reject the works of the devil in our lives by utilizing the grace attributes of the Kingdom of God against him. For example, when he attempts to hurt us by prompting someone we love to reject us, we respond in grace by forgiving that person and thereby making no effect the purpose the devil had in mind. The practice is, we love those who do not love us, we forgive those who do not forgive us, we enlarge our circle and accept those who reject us, we show kindness to those who are unkind, and we show mercy to those who do not extend mercy to us. This applies across the spectrum of the Kingdom of God. As we develop this attitude against all the wiles of the devil we walk in the freedom of our Kingdom. The principle is outlined in Romans 12:21, "Do not be overcome by evil, but overcome evil with good."

The devil is actively utilizing all his resources to entice, coerce, deceive, and lead humans to perform all manner of evil. He is the instigator of atrocities, wars, disasters, and all types of inhumanities. He infiltrates governments, learning institutions, churches, religious bodies, and entertainment industries at all levels in his efforts to oppose all that God declares to be righteous and holy.

God's divine plan for the redemption of mankind included Jesus taking back from the devil the authority that Adam had forfeited. He defeated the devil and made a public spectacle of him by exercising this authority over him. Jesus introduced a Kingdom where the love, grace, goodness, and righteousness of God were powerful weapons against His enemy.

Jesus demonstrated this Kingdom by counteracting the devil's evil deeds with the more powerful attributes of His Kingdom, thereby destroying the works of the devil. By introducing these aspects of His Kingdom to those who were willing to believe in Him, He armed them with the weapons to overcome the devil.

Jesus accomplished for mankind everything that was needed for redemption. When a person believes in Christ, he is born again with a new spirit capable of exercising authority over the demonic realm by ordering his life by the higher grace essentials of the Kingdom of God.

Colossians 2:15- Having <u>disarmed</u> principalities and powers, He made a public spectacle of them, triumphing over them in it.
- This is the reality expressed in I John 3:8. When a spiritual principality is disarmed it no longer has weapons to bring against Christians. It must resort to all manner of evil and subtle tactics to deceive them into believing he has power to control them. He cannot make them sin, but he can deceive them with a bombardment of thoughts that tempt them and influence wrong actions and attitudes.
- Romans 6:14 – For sin shall not have dominion over you, for you are not under law but under grace.
- Isaiah 54:17 – No weapon formed against you shall prosper and every tongue which rises against you in judgment you shall condemn.
- I Peter 5:8 – Be sober, be vigilant; because your adversary the devil walks about like a roaring lion, seeking whom he may devour.
- I Peter 5:9 - Resist him, steadfast in <u>the faith</u>, knowing that the same sufferings are experienced by your brotherhood in the world.

- Satan tries to disguise himself like a roaring lion, using this method to present himself as a powerful enemy that comes to damage and destroy. But since he has already been disarmed this is only a scare tactic to cause fear, and to intimidate the Christian. Peter advises us to be aware of this and to resist him steadfastly in the faith. In other words, don't let him pull the wool over our eyes.
- We see this same ploy used by Goliath when he stood before the army of Israel. He used his size, voice, and fighting expertise to ridicule and intimidate the army of Israel. But David was not deceived by his size or his intimidating tactics. He relied upon his relationship with God and slew the giant. We stand in the faith of what Jesus has done and who we are in Him.

II Corinthians 10:3-6 – For though we walk in the flesh, we do not war according to the flesh.

4- For the weapons of our warfare are not carnal but mighty in God for pulling down strongholds
5 - casting down arguments and every high thing that exalts itself against the knowledge of God, bringing every thought into captivity to the obedience of Christ.
6 - and being ready to punish all disobedience when your obedience is fulfilled.
- Because of our sensory inputs from the physical world we are acutely influenced by the activities of the world system, a system which is largely dominated by demonic forces. We are educated to respond to others in the same manner they use against us. When we forget that even though we are in the world that we are not of the world, we become conformed to the world system in which we live. Paul reminds us that the battle is not a physical one but our struggle is against a spiritual adversary.

- He states that our weaponry is spiritual with the potential of pulling down strongholds. Strongholds are those thought patterns and false-belief systems that are built on deception and error that have developed over time. They strongly hold us in bondage to ungodly attitudes and actions. These areas consists of those defense systems we hide behind to excuse our behavior, addictions, developed habits, atheism, and false religious belief that are contrary to Biblical teaching. Examples of strongholds are: habitual lying, alcoholism, pornography, unbiblical theology, unfounded fear, and uncontrolled anger. False beliefs in themselves do not constitute a stronghold. False beliefs become strongholds when they exercise control over major responses to life issues. Renewing the mind in these areas is essential to our freedom from them.

- It would follow that the weapon that would pull down a stronghold of a false belief is the truth of the Scriptures that sets one free. The weapon of one's true identity in Christ will pull downs those strongholds of inferiority and addiction. The gospel of grace is the antidote that frees from all bondages.

The exercise of these weapons is outlined in Romans 12:9-21. For example, verse nine states, "Let love be without hypocrisy." Hypocritical love professes to love God but hates another for whatever the reason. True agape love will expose and defeat a hypocritical love.

- It should be understood that spiritual warfare is first and foremost for the welfare and good of the individual. It is doubtful that the individual will experience spiritual warfare success in any arena where he has not first experienced it in his own life.

- Ephesians 6:10-17 – Finally, my brethren, be strong in the Lord and in the power of His might.

11- Put on the whole armor of God, that you may be able to <u>stand</u> against the wiles of the devil.

12- For we do not wrestle against flesh and blood, but against principalities, against powers, against the rulers of the darkness of this age, against spiritual host of wickedness in the heavenly places.

13- Therefore take up the whole armor of God, that you may be able to <u>withstand</u> in the evil day, and having done all, <u>to stand.</u>

14- <u>Stand</u> therefore, having girded your waist with the truth, having put on the breastplate of righteousness.

15- And having shod your feet with the preparation of the gospel of peace;

16- Above all, taking the shield of faith with which you will be able to quench all the fiery darts of the wicked one.

17- And take the helmet of salvation, and the sword of the Spirit, which is the word of God.

18- Praying always with all prayer and supplication in the Spirit, being watchful to this end with all perseverance and supplication for all the saints.

- In these verses Paul outlines the dynamics and the attitudes of spiritual warfare. The overriding instruction is to "stand." Paul does not mention anywhere in these verses that we are to fight, to enter into hand-to- hand combat with the devil when he attempts to wrestle from us those things given to us by God. No human could overpower Satan or his demons in a physical wrestling match, therefore the wrestling must take place in the mind. The mind is the battle ground, so bringing every thought into captivity to the obedience of Christ is essential to our victory. Nowhere in Scriptures does it state that Jesus got into a fist fight or a physical wrestling match with the devil. Neither did He use any of the tactics that many use today as spiritual warfare.

- When we examine the armor we find that each piece represents an area in which we are to stand. As we stand in truth we foil the lies of the enemy. When we stand in righteousness we defeat the attacks of unrighteousness. When we stand in the preparation of the gospel of peace we dispel false religious teachings. When we stand in faith we reject the ways of the world, flesh, and devil. By standing in our salvation, we stand in who God says we are and defeat rejection and all accusations of inferiority. When we stand in the word of God, we take the offense by actively using the word to present the truth about God, His grace, and His Kingdom. By doing so, we expose false beliefs, false gods, and erroneous ways of salvation for man.

- Paul closes by stressing the importance of the role of prayer in spiritual warfare. Prayer is to always be done in coordination with the Holy Spirit, with a compassion and concern for others and their needs that only God can provide. It is certainly proper to bombard demonic strongholds with prayer that expresses the will of God for those areas. Most spiritual breakthroughs do not come as a result of casual praying but only after one has persevered with determination.

I Timothy 6:12 – Fight the good <u>fight of faith</u>, lay hold on eternal life, to which you were also called and have confessed the good confession in the presence of many witnesses.
- The key in this verse is that the good fight is a fight of standing in faith. Faith believes in what Christ has already accomplished, what He will do, and who we are in Him.

II Timothy 4:7 – I have fought the good fight, I have finished the race, I have <u>kept the faith</u>.
- Paul again associates the good fight with having kept the faith.

II Chronicles 20:17 – You will not need to fight in this battle. Position yourselves, stand still and see the salvation of the LORD, who is with you, O Judah and Jerusalem! Do not fear or be dismayed; tomorrow go out against them for the LORD is with you.

- This is an Old Testament account where God's people exercised their faith by singing the praise of God before their enemies. The result was they never had to lift a weapon against their enemies and it took them three days to haul away the spoils of war left behind.
- One of the greatest weapons of our arsenal is passionate, unashamed worship of our King.

Romans 12:2 – And do not be conformed to this world, but be transformed by the renewing of your mind, that you may prove what is that good and acceptable and perfect will of God.

- The key to preparation for spiritual warfare is to have the mind of Christ when involved with the struggles and wiles of the devil. This is acquired through the renewing of the mind to think as He does in all matters (I Corinthians 2:16, Philippians 2:5, Philippians 4:8).

It is my belief that demons cannot posses a Christian. A demon cannot possess or own something that is God's. Neither would a demon want to live in the same house as the Holy Spirit. Jesus cast out many demons but never from an individual who was born again.

The enemies that we face in spiritual warfare are the devil, the flesh, and the world. We should always be mindful that regardless of how they may present themselves, these are always, always, our enemies. Each of these enemies has its own methods of enticing mankind away from the Kingdom life that God designed them to have. These enemies wreak havoc across a wide spectrum from simple deception to the atrocities experienced around the world, resulting in all manner of sickness, destruction, damaged relationships, wars, division, and the creation of all manner of religions that oppose God's plan of salvation for mankind.

There are several factors that are important in defeating these enemies. First, the Christian must know his true identity in Christ, must arm himself with knowledge of the Bible, and have an active relationship with the Holy Spirit. Second, he must be acutely aware of the tactics of each of these enemies. It is the truths of the gospel that free us from each of them.

In Romans 8:31-36 Paul sets forth such a solid case for the Christian's position before God that there is no rational defense against it. He starts with the obvious, that if God is for us who can be against us? Who can prevail over God?

- Paul then emphatically declares that if God loves us so much that He sent His Son to die for us, how would such a God then withhold any good thing from us.
- God has already justified us, so who has the right to bring any charges against us?
- Since Christ died for us, has risen, and sits at the right hand of God interceding for us, what right does anyone have to condemn us? It is obvious that God does not condemn us.
- Regardless of hurtful and harmful encounters in our lives there is nothing that can stop God from loving us.
- Knowing this gives us a powerful weapon against the assaults of the devil.

Romans 8:37 – Yet in all these things we are more than conquerors through Him who loves us.

- Paul declares that regardless of the encounters we are more than conquerors over all these things. Not that we must fight to overcome them but that we are already conquerors through Christ. (I Corinthians 15:57).
- I John 5:4 – For whatever is born of God overcomes the world. And this is the victory that has overcome the world – <u>our faith.</u>
- I John 4:4 – You are of God, little children, and have overcome them, because He who is in you is greater than he who is in the world.
- John 16:33 – These things I have spoken to you, that in Me you may have peace, in the world you will have tribulation, but be of good cheer, <u>I have overcome the world.</u>

- I John 3:8 – He who sins is of the devil, for the devil has sinned from the beginning. For this purpose the Son of God was manifested, that He might <u>destroy the works of the devil.</u>
- Galatians 5:16 – I say then; Walk in the Spirit, and you shall not fulfill the lust of the flesh.

These Scriptures make it abundantly clear that in Christ we have the power over the world, flesh, and devil.

Immediately after His anointing by the Holy Spirit at his water baptism, Jesus was led into the wilderness to face the temptations of the devil on our behalf. He fasted for forty days and nights. After prolonged times of fasting the body will begin to feed on its muscle tissue for energy. Jesus was faced with this possibility when He became hungry. The devil often uses the fear of our individual state of wellbeing to panic us into doing something contrary to faith having the power over the world, flesh, and devil (Matthew 3:16-17, Matthew 4:1-11).

The first thing the devil did was to attack Jesus' identity. The Father had declared that Jesus was His beloved Son therefore the devil starts his first temptation with the statement, "If You are the Son of God." Notice he left out "beloved." This was an attempt to get Jesus to doubt who He was. This has been a strategy the devil has used through the generations attacking the validity of who we are in Christ. Secondly, he attempts to get Jesus to use His position to satisfy a personal necessity. Thirdly, he once again tried to get Jesus to prove that He is the Son of God by committing a willful, harmful act to prove God's word. Fourthly, he tried to tempt Jesus by offering Him all the fallen kingdoms of the world. He was attempting to distract Jesus in His weakened stage from believing that He alone was the King over the only true Kingdom, the Kingdom of God. The devil was tempting Him as he also tempts us, to give up something that is permanent for something that is temporary. His objective was to get Jesus to worship him. It is obvious that he has succeeded in deceiving the world into doing this very thing as is evidenced by the many false religions on earth. (I Corinthians 10:20-21)

It is a sad indictment that all of these have been effective against Christians from the garden to present time. Jesus stood fast in who He knew Himself to be, and used the truth of God's word as His offensive weapon. When He said, "Man shall not live by bread alone, but by every word that proceeds from the mouth of God," He was revealing that God speaks into every area of our lives. Unless He has directed us to proceed in a matter we should not proceed. Jesus walked upon the water but it would be foolish for a non-swimmer to step out of the boat in deep water without being assured that was what God wanted him to do. I would venture to say that through the years many have attempted to walk on water, but to date, other than Peter, I have no personal knowledge that any have succeeded. It was not that Jesus could not turn the rocks into bread, but He only did what the Father directed and He had not directed Him so. He later did get the word to miraculously feed five thousand and obeyed.

In summary, spiritual warfare is not an attempt to defeat Satan and his emissaries because Jesus has already defeated them; it is fighting the good fight by standing in faith whenever accosted by the world, flesh, and Satan. We must stand by faith in who Christ is, stand by faith in who we are, and stand by faith in the finished work of all that Jesus has done.

Since strongholds and sinful habits are the result of a violation of some characteristic of the Kingdom of God, they must be replaced by the characteristic they violate. Strongholds and debilitating habits in an individual's life are overcome by the renewing of the mind to truth regarding those areas. Lying is replaced by speaking the truth, unforgiveness is replaced by compassion, and rejection is replaced by the knowledge that God loves and accepts. Strongholds of sin are replaced with the knowledge that sin does not have dominion because of the power of the indwelling Holy Spirit and the righteousness of our new nature.

The demonic control over cities and nations is overcome by penetrating the area with the attributes of the Kingdom of God. Preparation for this is to saturate the area with spiritual prayer for those affected. The ruling principle is that light always dispels darkness.

The objective of spiritual warfare is always to present the reality of the Kingdom of God as the antidote for mankind's need. Successful spiritual warfare is accomplished by believing and living in our true identity and position in Christ, knowing that Jesus defeated the devil, being aware of the tactics of demons, and worshipping God with unashamed passion.

CHAPTER SIX

The Church

The Church is not the Kingdom but is an essential part of the Kingdom because its function is to promote the fundamentals of the Kingdom here on earth. The Church accomplishes this by nurturing, training, equipping, educating, and providing a grace atmosphere where its members can mature into their roles in the Kingdom of God and enjoy the benefits of the New Covenant.

The Church was birthed on the day of Pentecost with the coming of the role of the Holy Spirit. Jesus had instructed His disciples to wait in Jerusalem until they received power from on high (Luke 24:49). He tells them they would receive this power when the Holy Spirit came upon them and then they would be empowered to be His witnesses as a lifestyle (Acts 1:8). They were already "saved" because Jesus had already breathed on them and told them to, "Receive the Holy Spirit," (John 20:22). Paul states, "But you are not in the flesh but in the Spirit, if indeed the Spirit of God dwells in you," (Romans 8:9). It is the ministry of the Holy Spirit to baptize us into the body of Christ, the Church (I Corinthians 12:13, Ephesians 1:22-23).

The Church must develop and maintain an atmosphere of grace where the tenets of the New Covenant can be taught, demonstrated, and practiced at all age levels by its members. The Church is to provide a safe haven for all people, a place where hurting and dysfunctional individuals can come for safety and healing. The Church earnestly protects the grace atmosphere where all feel accepted regardless of their situation or need. Through its teaching and training the Church guides its member in maturing into the person God has designed them to be. The Church does this by helping its members to develop their identity in Christ and by making them aware of the ministry of the Holy Spirit to empower them to manifest grace lives. The Church will assist individuals in recognizing and developing their spiritual gifts through teaching, demonstrating, and by providing an atmosphere and opportunity where they can exercise their giftings.

The Church must provide a platform for unashamed, passionate, corporate worship where individuals may express their love and gratefulness to God. Passionate worship is encouraged by the example of passionate worship leaders. Pastors as well as other church leaders help to establish the atmosphere of worship by their enthusiastic participation. The church should allow and encourage all Biblical expressions of worship.

The Church will take seriously the ministry of reconciliation that Jesus has assigned His church. It will teach its membership their responsibility of telling the lost world of God's great love in reconciling them to Himself. The ministry of reconciliation must be practiced by the church and the individual in the whole spectrum of relationships. It is closely associated with the role of peacemaker. It is important that each individual be assured that his/her sins have been forgiven and that they communicate this truth to the save and unsaved alike (Acts 1:8, II Corinthians 5:18-19).

The Church will hold seriously as one of its goals to lead its members is to, "Grow in the grace and knowledge of our Lord and Savior Jesus Christ," (II Peter 3:18). This will be accomplished by rightly dividing the Scriptures to extract their truths as the means of a constant renewing of the mind.

The Church will instruct its congregation about the purpose, the process, and the joy of living in the realm of grace. The Scriptures outline this purpose and process.

- Ephesians 2:10 – For we are His workmanship created in Christ Jesus for good works, which God prepared beforehand that we should walk in them.
  - o God created us for a divine purpose to accomplish good works and made all the necessary provisions so that we could walk in these good works and enjoy them.
- For we are God's own handiwork, (His workmanship), recreated in Christ Jesus (born anew), that we may do those good works which God predestined (planned beforehand) for us (taking paths which He prepared ahead of time), that we should walk in them—living the good life which He prearranged and made ready for us to live (Ephesians 2:10, Amplified Bible).
- Philippians 2:13 – For it is God who works in you both to will and do for His good pleasure.
  - o God has taken the responsibility of revealing His will to us, and then to empower us to do that will. God reveals the good works we are to do and provides us the means to accomplish them.
- Philippians 1:6 – Being confident of this very thing, that He who has begun a good work in you will complete it until the day of Jesus Christ.
  - o God's work in us is a progressive work of growing in the grace and knowledge of God by revealing the truths of His Kingdom so that our minds are always in the state of being renewed.
- Acts 1:8 – But you shall receive power when the Holy Spirit has come upon you; and you shall be witnesses to Me in Jerusalem, and in all Judea and Samaria, and to the end of the world.
  - o The Holy Spirit leads us into all truth, reveals the good works we are to be involved in, and empowers us to accomplish them. Our loving Father has left nothing to chance.

- Philippians 4:13 – I can do all things through Christ who strengthens me.
  o We can say with confidence that we are able to accomplish everything that He requires of us that pertains to the good works of the Kingdom because we were created to do them.

The Church will administer discipline when it becomes necessary for the good of the congregation and the affected individual. The purpose for church discipline is always to restore the person involved. Excommunication becomes necessary only if the person refuses to be restored and/or tries to influence others to his/her deviant lifestyle. The church must never allow one person to remain in the fellowship to the detriment of the congregation at large. One bad apple should not be allowed to spoil the whole barrel.

Since grace is the very backbone of a developing church it is difficult to understand why some who say they embrace the grace of God reject their fundamental responsibilities in helping others mature in the tenets of grace by refusing to participate in a local church. When one who professes to understand grace uses the imperfections and immaturities of churches and their leaders as the reason/excuse to stop attending all churches, he is no longer walking in the very grace he professes. How can anyone who professes grace reject association with the very people who are the bride of Christ? The excuse that no church provides them adequate spiritual help fails to measure up when examined by real grace. Since all Christians are the "Church," how can one reject his duties as a part of the church? This does not appear to be a New Covenant reason for not attending church. Failure to associate with a local congregation because of a superior knowledge about grace would appear to be spiritual pride and a pseudo-grace. This is not to say that one should remain in a local congregation that refuses to allow him to express his beliefs in the gospel of grace. The writer of the book of Hebrews entreats us to consider one another in order to stir up love and good works, not forsaking the assembling or ourselves together, as the manner of some, but exhorting one another (Hebrews 10:24-25).

One grace plant in a church congregation can bear fruit that has a positive effect on many others in that congregation. If those who understand the importance of grace extract themselves from any involvement with a local church who will demonstrate to those in the church true grace? The very essence of grace is to draw larger circles to include those that do not embrace the Biblical teachings of grace.

It must be understood that these are the functions of an ideal church and that the local church will always be in the process of developing these functions. The Church, like the individual, is in a constant mode of change to become what Christ describes it to be. When a church seeks to establish a grace atmosphere in its congregation many of these functions will fall naturally into place. The Bride of Christ, the true Church, is much like the woman described in Proverbs 31. She honors her Husband by her virtuous acts of love expressed through her responsibilities to Him.

CHAPTER SEVEN

The Favor of God

One of the most astounding verses in the Bible about the most amazing person of the Bible, for me, is Luke 2:52. For one to believe that the Son of God restricted Himself to the human process of growth wherein as He grew in stature that He also had to grow in wisdom is perhaps understandable. But to comprehend that He grew in favor with God, as well as men, is more difficult for me to get my mind around.

Luke 2:52 – "And Jesus increased in wisdom and stature, and in favor with God and men."

Jesus never modeled the Church per se, He modeled the Kingdom of God. Every encounter that Jesus had was a divine encounter. Today we call it a divine encounter when it is obvious that God set it up. We have all experienced these encounters. Since Jesus only did what the Father told Him to do every encounter He had was a divine encounter. Every person that Jesus interacted with during these encounters represented the thousands of others around the world with similar problems and needs, and God's willingness to meet those needs.

The story about the life of Jesus recorded in Luke 2:41-50 unveils a portion of His life as a young boy. It allows us to see the strong desire that Jesus had even as a boy to be about the Father's business, the things of the Father. The preceding verse (Luke 2:40) says that as He grew as a child He became mighty in spirit, and that He was filled with wisdom and the grace of God was upon Him. This did not happen just because He was the Son of God. It was a lifestyle that He practiced. The father and mother chosen by God to be His earthly parents were godly examples who taught and encouraged Him through the formative years of His life.

They certainly helped to establish His identity by constantly reminding Him of the events surrounding His birth, and by stressing that God was His Father. They taught Him the Scriptures and provided Him with spiritual guidance, but Jesus Himself had to make the decisions in His everyday activities to be obedient to His earthly authority as well as His heavenly Father.

Jesus was born during the four-hundred-year period when there were no prophets speaking for God and into a religious system that had deteriorated because it was without divine guidance. We have to give His parents credit for the spiritual influence they had in His early life. Yet, in the midst of this fallen generation Jesus impacted the world as no other has ever done, leaving us the example that our spirituality does not depend upon the religious climate around us.

Jesus demonstrated by his questions and interaction with the leaders of the Temple that He had an insatiable appetite for spiritual matters even as a growing child. Certainly His parents had a major role in feeding this appetite. Children in their early stage of development are very vulnerable to the actions, attitudes, and words of the adults around them, especially their parents. It is the parents' role to guide and guard them as they acquire all types of knowledge from the many sources to which they are exposed.

God chose Mary and Joseph to be His earthly parents because He knew He could trust them to reinforce in Jesus the things that would help Him become mighty in spirit. It was no wonder that He stayed behind discussing spiritual things with the leaders of the Temple, asking questions regarding these things.

The question that entered my mind, as pointless as it might be, was, "Where did Jesus spend the night when he remained behind those three days?" The Bible does not say that He had kinfolks there to stay with so where would you think He stayed? Well, we really don't know for sure but I believe the Scriptures shed some light.

Luke 21:37 – And in the daytime He was teaching in the temple, but at night He went out and stayed on the mountain called Olivet.

Luke 22:39 – Coming out, He went to the Mount of Olives, <u>as He was accustomed</u>, and His disciples also followed Him.

John 7:53-8:1 – And everyone went to his own house but Jesus went to the Mount of Olives.

I suggest that He may have started going there when He was twelve to pray, and ponder what He had learned in the Temple that day. Finding it a quiet, secluded place where He could meet with the Father, He would later continue to go there to pray. We know that in His growth process He learned to pray because as an adult He spent much time in prayer and one of His favorite places was the Mount of Olives. He developed His obedience to the voice of God at a young age, and purposed in His heart to do whatever the Father directed Him to do regardless.

I have some difficulty fully understanding how He, as God, restricted Himself to the vulnerability and the same growth stages that each of us had to grow through. How could a God so big restrict Himself to an embryo? I realize that He did this so that He could experience everything that we experience. Knowing that He chose to go though a nine-months growth in the womb and develop through all the different stages so he could identify with me, does help me better understand His great love for me.

I have no difficulty believing that Jesus grew in favor with people.

- <u>With His earthly parents</u>. Certainly He would have been a joy and a blessing to them as they watched Him mature through each stage of His life. He would have grown in their favor.
- <u>Widow of Nain</u>. This poor lady had already lost her husband, now her son. In despair and grief she was on her way to bury this one she loved when this astonishing man intersects her life with restored hope. This young man was dead therefore he had some afterlife experience; he had experienced the glories of Paradise or the fires of Hell. His reaction to being brought back to life is one of the many unrecorded events of Jesus' life. We do know that this remarkable Savior by divine appointment gave him a second chance with life. We can only imagine the depth of gratitude that flooded the heart of this mother at the recovery of her son, and we can say with full assurance that in her eyes Jesus surely grew in her favor (<u>Luke 7:11-17</u>). She represents the many that face impossible situations that have had their hopes restored by Jesus.
- <u>Demoniac of Gadara</u> – These Scriptures picture a man who represents the myriad of lost, hurting people in every century. He is tormented, hopelessly lost, wandering in the graveyard among the dead. He is beyond help from family or friend. Tormented and driven by demons he is without hope of recovery. He is representative of those who are desperately lost, driven by forces they cannot control. Then Jesus arrives on the scene by divine appointment and frees him from his dilemma. His sanity is restored, he once again has a life, and he can return to his family and friends as a whole person. It is obvious from his response that Jesus grew in his favor that wonderful day (Mark 5:10-20).
- <u>Woman with a blood issue</u> – She has an incurable problem and no hope of being healed. She has exhausted her finances

on medical help that has provided no relief. When she hears about Jesus, evidently His compassion and willingness to heal, she concludes that if she can just touch his garment she will be made well, and she was. She represents those with incurable diseases and unfixable problems that need a divine appointment with this Physician. With the experiencing of this miracle Jesus certainly grew in her favor (Mark 5:25-34).

- <u>Blind man</u> – This man had suffered the anguish of blindness every day for forty years. He had never enjoyed seeing a sunset, blue sky, blooming flowers, and the like. He had surely been hurt by conversations overheard from those passing by, such as Jesus' disciples when they tried to diagnose the cause of his blindness. Then Jesus gave him sight; he was introduced to a whole new world or wonder and awe, a divine appointment. He represents all the millions who are spiritually blinded that Jesus wishes to introduce to a whole new world. I imagine with each new wonder Jesus grew in his favor (John 9:1-41).

- <u>Women at the well</u> – Having failed to find love and acceptance in five unsuccessful marriages she was now living with someone outside of marriage. Her choices had certainly gained her a reputation in the village. She probably went to draw water at a time when she would not have to encounter the other women. Instead, she had a divine appointment with the Messiah. He did not condemn her but instead promised her living water that would provide her with everlasting life. She represents the thousands who are suffering because of failed relationships. This life-changing knowledge from such a person would have caused Him to grow in her favor (John 4:4-26).

- <u>My Daughter</u> – Several years ago my daughter was diagnosed with cancer. Although she chose to receive the treatment her doctor recommended, her trust was in the faithfulness of God believing that what He has done for others He would also do for her. He healed her! Now each time yearly tests verify that the cancer is still gone, through gratitude, Jesus grows in her favor.

If I knew your story I am sure it could be included here, also. But how He, the Son of God, could increase in the favor of the Father who loved Him, my finite mind must probe for a greater revelation to find an answer that I can grasp.

Before the beginning Jesus was in complete union with the Father and the Holy Spirit as part of the Trinity. His creativity was expressed throughout the scope of creation. He took part in the divine plans for the redemption of man all prior to the creation of man. He was slain before the foundation of the world for the sake of mankind. Before He had healed any sick or performed any miracles the Father says at His water baptism that He is well-pleased with Him (Matthew 3:17).

Again on the Mount of Transfiguration the Father affirms that He is well-pleased with His beloved Son. There does not seem to be a time when the Father was not well-pleased with Him so to grasp the fact that Jesus grew in God's favor does take a little pondering. It should be understood here that the operative word is "favor" and not love, because the love of God for His Son and for us has never been anything but maximum and extended unconditionally.

What is the conclusion? I have concluded that perhaps what is meant is that God was able to release more favor as Jesus matured through each stage of His life. A father does not show favor to a five-year-old by allowing him the use of the family car. In a similar manner there are favors of God that are only released as we mature enough to rightly appreciate and employ them. The question arises as how does a person secure more favor from God?

We could start by looking into the life of Jesus. On several occasions Jesus stated that He only did what the Father told Him to do or what He saw the Father doing. This expresses two important necessities, actively listening to God and knowing His voice, and having a mindset of doing what God says to do. Jesus' life is a demonstration of how we are to live. Modeling our lives after His will assure the same favor He received.

Jesus shares His secret (perhaps a better word would be His means) in Matthew 4:4 where He emphatically declares that man must live by every word that proceeds from the mouth of God. Think of His case for a moment. He was in a vulnerable situation, being strongly tempted by the devil, a situation that most of us find ourselves in at some time or other. It is in the midst of this situation that Jesus proclaims His secret of resisting the devil while simultaneously assuring favor from God—just listen to God and do what He says.

It is a given that for one to live by what God says, He must hear God, and for one to hear God he must set a precedence of listening to God. Whatever God says to an individual will be something that will provide guidance and revelation for his life.

There is Scripture in the Old Testament that gives us insight into how one may develop a time to actively listen to God. Moses set up a "Tent of Meeting" outside the camp away from distractions where individuals could go and meet with God. It is assumed since Moses talked with God in the tent about current matters that the purpose for the tent was to provide a place where the Israelites could meet with God in private, without distraction, and seek guidance in their life matters (Exodus 33:7-11). In the New Testament Jesus provides us with a similar model. He says when we pray we should find a place where we can be free of distractions and meet with God in private (Matthew 6:6). The obvious teaching here is that He wants personal time with us where He has our undivided attention because what He says is of the utmost importance to our lives.

Spiritual maturity, i.e., the process of developing into the person that God declares us to be, is both a physical and spiritual process. We grow physically while simultaneously acquiring valuable knowledge that helps us maintain our lives in a physical world. But we also live in a spiritual kingdom where we acquire the knowledge to live in harmony with the spiritual principles of this kingdom. In the one case we have teachers of various kinds that lead us into acquiring the knowledge and skills we need to be successful in the physical realm. In the other case it is the Holy Spirit who teaches us the ways, means, and conduct of the Kingdom and provides us with the grace to be in union with others in the kingdom.

In our formal education we attend classes and read text books and in our spiritual education the Holy Spirit uses life situations and the Scriptures to teach us. We find these guiding texts throughout the Scriptures and go to the Spirit for understanding. One such Scripture is II Peter 1:2-8. These verses outline how we are to response to encounters, situations, thoughts, and circumstances that we face throughout each day of our lives. The objective is for us to apply the spiritual ethics of the Kingdom when we are confronted with the ideas, actions, and attitudes of the world system.

As we do so we increase in favor with God because we assume our responsibilities in the Kingdom of God. Verses five through eight give us guideposts for maturing as we apply these in our daily encounters.

- <u>Faith</u> – Throughout our day we are faced with situations that require a faith response.
- <u>Virtue</u> – Moral excellence. Responding with virtue when we are tempted toward immorality.
- <u>Knowledge</u> – The acquiring of the truths as outlined in the Scriptures (II Peter 3:18).
- <u>Self-control</u> – One of the fruits of the Spirit that indicates we are responding from our spirit man rather than the flesh.
- <u>Perseveran</u>ce – Developing the mindset of an overcomer.
- <u>Godliness</u>   - Pious mindset that govern our actions.
- <u>Brotherly Kindness</u> - Not being selective in who we express love toward.
- <u>Love</u> – Developing an unconditional love toward all mankind.

Hindrances to favor with God

A.   Being offended toward God.
     Matthew 11:1-12 – Luke 7:18-35
     John was in prison because He was doing what God had
     called him to do. He surely did not expect such an important
     ministry would land him in prison. He had declared Jesus
     to be the Son of God that would take away the sins of the
     world, and now he was suffering because of his ministry. John
     was entertaining the doubts that have plagued most of us in
     ministry when we feel we have done what God required of us
     and things still go badly. When we hold God accountable for
     allowing bad things to happen in our lives it causes our faith
     in Him to weaken. When our faith is weakened we begin to
     doubt the faithfulness of God and this hinders Him from
     releasing favor toward us.
     We may also allow unanswered questions toward God to cause
     us to be offended toward Him.
          Why did God allow_____?
          Why did God allow John to be beheaded?
          Why did God allow those in Hebrews 11:30-40 to be
          killed in horrible ways?
     Life is full of unanswered questions. If we must have all our
     questions answered before we can trust God we will miss out
     on many acts of His favor. I don't understand how pictures and
     sounds can be transmitted over airwaves but I am not going
     to refuse to watch TV until I fully understand.
     It is okay to admit we don't know the whys and the ways of
     God, and why things happen as they do. Perhaps some things
     are on a need-to-know basis. But we can live by what we do
     know, God is good. He has proven this by sending His Son to
     die for us and so He can shower us with His favor. His word is
     full of promises for us to receive. This we know! We know He
     is always good and righteous in all that He does. We should
     never allow any teaching or any person that depict God as a

harsh, unloving God to influence us away from the fact that God is love!

B. Living a carnal lifestyle
Carnality leads to dullness in our ability to hear the Holy Spirit. The basis of our faith is in our ability to hear the Spirit. If we are unable to hear the Spirit we will live our lives based upon carnal decisions in life situations (Hebrews 5:11-13).

Carnality can only tolerate milk, an indication that the person is still in an infant stage and not able to exercise the accountability necessary to receive many favors of God that come only through maturity (I Corinthians 3:1-7).

Carnality is worldly responses that oppose Kingdom responses in our maturing process, and hinders the favor of God in those areas (II Peter 1:5-8).

Carnality is attempting to live under the laws of the Old Covenant or a mixture of the Old and New covenants. This causes the person to fall from grace because they choose to depend on what he can do rather than trusting in what God has already done (Galatians 5:1-4).

Jesus came that we might have life, and have it more abundantly, that we might receive the full favor of God. The Holy Spirit tutors us through our process of maturing so that we are prepared to receive more of God's favors at each stage. God has chosen to love us and show us favor but in His wisdom He does not entrust us with things that we are not spiritually mature enough to manage.

Chapter Eight

The good seed of the Kingdom

The difficult times in our lives provide us with means to gain maturity and become fruitful as we view them as opportunities to exercise grace. When we view difficult times as somehow being God's fault or the devil's power over us, we develop a victim's mentality, lose our faith in the goodness of God, become discouraged, abort God's purpose for our lives, and reject His placement for our ministry. We are faced with choices on a daily basis. Many of these choices are made based upon our commitment as a Christian and often carry consequences contrary to our comfort and well-being because they conflict with the ways of the world system.

I firmly believe that it is God's will for Christians to penetrate this world system of unbelief, moral deterioration, racism, prejudiced division, and selfishness with the mind-set that the people who live contrary to the ways of God are not our problem but our very purpose. God is not so much concerned about what a lost world thinks about Christmas as He is about what Christians are doing to prove the reality of His Kingdom. A lost person had much rather find the relief from his sicknesses and insurmountable problems that Jesus offers rather than hold to an atheistic or agnostic belief about God. The world is waiting for Christians to rightly represent the God they profess.

It is our responsibility, and should be our desire, to represent the Kingdom of God with all its benefits and blessings to those that are living without this knowledge. Our primary ministry as we interact with those in our world is to accurately and clearly live the message before them that God was in Christ reconciling them to Himself. We must approach this with the understanding that God has provided us with the grace to be able to accomplish this even in the midst of the difficulties that we will face in our everyday lives. As the sons of the Kingdom we are planted in the world as good seed with a divine purpose.

In Matthew 13:36-43 Where Jesus explains the parable of the tares. He states that He is the sower, the field is the world, the good seeds are the sons of the Kingdom, and the tares are the sons of the devil. The sower sows with a purpose, He never sows bad seed, and He sows with an expectation.

The world has no power over its condition and is therefore in dire need of the product produced by the seed. The tares are the counterfeits that the devil plants wherever the good seed is planted in order to deceive the masses. Tares represent the followers of the false religions of the world, all those who exclude Jesus as the only means for man's salvation. It includes all those who have elevated their savior to be above or equal with the Son of God.

Through the ages tares have been strategically placed in the field of the world by the devil, to draw the masses away from the truth as given by God to mankind. The world will allow tares to grow by legitimizing their roles, while resisting the growth of the good seed in the same way that a garden will allow weeds to grow equally with good seed. It should be noted that the field (world) did not recognize the difference between the wheat and the tares, only the Sower and His true servants were able to tell the difference.

There are several things that we can surmise regarding the good seed. For it to be of value and productive, it must be planted. The good seed can only produce after its kind, never something different. In order for it to produce it must first die. The seed can not plant itself and must rely on the sower to plant it. The seed has the DNA of its source and has an innate propensity to grow into maturity and produce its fruit. The type of seed determines the length to its maturity. It has the capability to preserve through difficult times in order to live and produce.

When applying the good seed to the individual Christian we see there is a process of maturing and bearing fruit of like kind. The process of maturing requires stages of growth changes. In the Christian this embraces the constant process of the renewing of the mind (Romans 12:2). In the same manner that a seed needs water to grow properly, the Christian must be watered by the Word of God, both written and spoken.

Various Scriptures give understanding of the spiritual method of maturation. One such Scripture is II Peter 1:5-8 in which we find an outline of the maturing process. Just a casual meditation upon each of these daily life encounters will open our understanding that for the Christian to mature through these encounters he must respond positively to them. The Christian is constantly faced with situations that require a Biblical response in each of these areas. He is strengthened through each of these opportunities as he responds from his good seed DNA, i.e., situations that require faith are responded to with faith, those that require virtue with virtuous responses, and so throughout each of these listed. To fail to respond properly causes a hindrance to the maturing process.

Critical to the maturing process is for the Christian to have the proper mindset toward the thoughts and ideas entertained by his mind. We find valuable guidance and encouragement on how to accomplish this in Philippians 4:8. This Scripture gives us a starter list on which things we are to meditate on, and leaves us with the obvious understanding that we should not meditate on their opposites. In other words we can use this list to identify those thoughts that we should and should not meditate upon, if our thoughts are to be virtuous and praiseworthy. With the combination of II Peter 1:5-8 and Philippians 4:8 the Christian is armed with valuable guidelines for his maturing process. It should be understood that the end product that the seed produces was already determined by the source from which the seed came. It only matured into what it already was. As Christians we only mature into the person that God has said we are.

It has been my desire to help equip the serious Christian with some scriptural truths that will assist them in facing the multitude of life situations that they will encounter during their Christian pilgrimage. Please understand that these chapters are only intended to offer some basic insights for understanding our roles in the Kingdom of God and to provide some methods of recognizing the misinterpretation and misapplications of Scriptures. I trust these will be guide-posts that will help point you to deeper understanding of Scripture and a more meaningful walk in your Christian life.

Printed in the United States
By Bookmasters